KU-567-388

Great Britain

the land and its people

Anna Sproule

Macdonald Educational

LIBRARY
POLYTECHNIC

Contents

8   A land of rich variety

10   Languages and beliefs

12   The makings of the British

14   The monarchs of Britain

16   The British revolutions

18   Queen-Empress: the age of Queen
    Victoria

20   How Great Britain has changed

22   The arts past and present

24   Heroes of fact and fiction

26   Inventors and discoverers

28   What Britain has to sell

30   London: the capital city

32   Cloudy skies and green, green gardens

34   Homes and households

36   Eating the British way

38   Education in Britain

40   Time off: leisure and pleasure

42   Reference

43   Index

44   Political map of Great Britain

45   Physical map of Great Britain

A land of rich variety

Mountains, lakes and coastlines

Great Britain is made up of three countries, England, Scotland and Wales. With Northern Ireland, it forms the United Kingdom.

It is a land of tremendous variety. Its landscapes range from mountains, lakes and forests, especially in Wales and Scotland, to flat plains, some of them below sea level. It contains the rolling pastoral country of central England and the bleak moorlands of Devon and Cornwall in the southwest. Some coastlines are rocky; others are lined with miles of sandy beaches. On Britain's highest peak, Ben Nevis in northwest Scotland, there may be snow for much of the year.

Visitors to Great Britain are often surprised by the wide variety in its countryside. They are also surprised by how small Britain is. But, with an average of 229 people living in each square kilometre, it is one of the most crowded countries in the world.

▲ The valley of Glencoe in the Scottish Highlands, the scene of the massacre of 38 people in 1692. It is an important centre for tourism and activities like climbing, walking and skiing.

▼ Visiting Britain by bicycle. In count areas, many people rely on their own transport just to go about their daily li Three-quarters of Britain is still thinly-populated open country.

▲ The London borough of Croydon is less thickly populated than some of the inner areas of London. But, with its population of over 300 000, it still has more people per square kilometre than most other areas in Britain.

Everyone in Britain probably knows at
[leas]t one area very well indeed: their own.
[But] the 14 million or so visitors who come
[to B]ritain every year may well have the
[bes]t idea of what the whole country really
[look]s like. The map shows just some of the
[thin]gs that interest them, from Scotland
[righ]t down to the south coast of England.

[SC]OTLAND
[1] [S]t Andrew's Cross, flag of Scotland.
[2] [T]artan of Macleod.
[3] [T]artan of Macgregor.
[4] [L]och Ness, home of the legendary
    [m]onster, near Inverness.
[5] ['B]onnie Prince Charlie' (Charles Stuart).
    [I]n 1745 he tried – unsuccessfully – to
    [m]ake himself king of Britain.
[6] [B]en Nevis, highest point in Britain
    [(1]341 m.).
[7] [S]cottish castle of the type found from
    [th]e Borders northwards.
[8] [O]il rig in the North Sea.

[NO]RTH ENGLAND
[9] Coin showing Britannia, issued by the
    Roman Emperor Hadrian.
[10] Hadrian's Wall at Haltcastle.
[11] The Venerable Bede, 'father of English
    history', worked at Jarrow.
[12] Holy Island (Lindisfarne), home of early
    Christian monks.
[13] Longstone Lighthouse and Grace
    Darling, who heroically rescued sailors
    from a sinking ship in 1838.

[EA]ST ANGLIA
[14] The tulip fields of Lincolnshire.
[15] Flat Fenland landscape.
[16] Windmills in Suffolk and Norfolk.
[17] Reed harvest in Norfolk.
[18] Thatchwork on a Norfolk cottage.

[TH]E MIDLANDS
[19] Warwickshire, home of Shakespeare.
[20] House of Tudor period, Stratford.
[21] Warwickshire landscape.
[22] Staffordshire, pottery centre.
[23] Oxford University.
[24] Great Tom Tower, Oxford.

[WA]LES
[25] Harlech Castle.
[26] National dress of Wales.
[27] The mountains of Snowdonia.
[28] The Welsh dragon, symbol of Wales.

[SO]UTHERN ENGLAND
[29] Oast houses for drying hops, Kent.
[30] Kent, 'garden of England'.
[31] Banner of the Cinque Ports.
[32] Dover Castle, Kent.
[33] South coast piers.
[34] White cliffs of Sussex and Kent.

[WE]ST COUNTRY
[35] Nineteenth-century tin mine.
[36] Tourist beaches in Cornwall.
[37] St Michael's Mount, Cornwall.
[38] The harbour of Polperro.

Languages and beliefs

Who are the people of Britain?

In 1981, when the last census count was held, there were 54 million Britons living in Great Britain. But very few of them would have called themselves that. The people of Britain tend to think of themselves not as British or Britons, but as English, Welsh, or Scottish.

Most of Britain's population comes from families that have lived somewhere in the country for many generations. Their main language is English – although some of them also speak the quite different Celtic languages of Welsh, Gaelic, Manx Gaelic, or Cornish. But some of the British come from families that have arrived in Britain since the Second World War. For example, their original family homes were in India, Pakistan, Bangladesh, in the West Indies or different parts of the Mediterranean, and many still speak the languages used there. The different religions of those who have settled in Britain also recall their countries of family origin, and include Islam and Hinduism. The majority religion of Britain is Christianity.

Lincoln Cathedral, one of the finest [reli]gious buildings in Great Britain. [The] traditional religion of Britain is [Chri]stianity. When Lincoln Cathedral was [beg]un, in 1072, British Christians were all [Rom]an Catholic. Now many belong to the [Prot]estant Churches, such as the Church [of E]ngland and the Church of Scotland.

[D]uring its history, Britain has exported [its m]ain language all over the world.

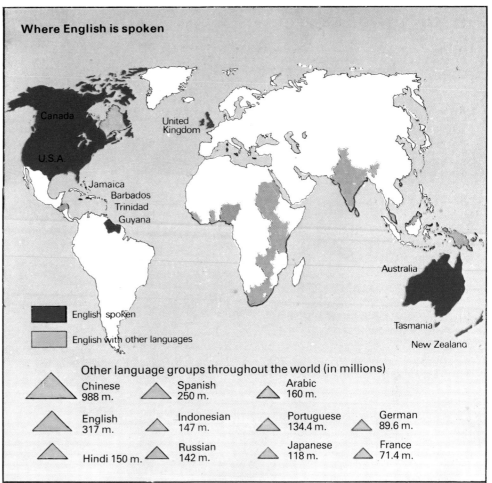

Where English is spoken

Canada

United Kingdom

U.S.A.

Jamaica
Barbados
Trinidad
Guyana

Australia

Tasmania

New Zealand

☐ English spoken

☐ English with other languages

Other language groups throughout the world (in millions)

Chinese 988 m.	Spanish 250 m.	Arabic 160 m.
English 317 m.	Indonesian 147 m.	Portuguese 134.4 m.	German 89.6 m.
Hindi 150 m.	Russian 142 m.	Japanese 118 m.	France 71.4 m.

[A] Londoner of West Indian descent [add]resses passers-by in Hyde Park. [Alth]ough his place of family origin is [tho]usands of miles away, his language, [like] that of his listeners, is English.

[From the early 1950s onwards, people [fro]m many countries in Asia, Africa and [the] West Indies came to Britain to find [wo]rk. They settled in British cities like [Lon]don and Birmingham. Many are [Mu]slims, and worship at mosques like [th]e one in London.

[Queen Elizabeth II with the Dean of [Wi]ndsor. Queen Elizabeth is head of the [Chu]rch of England, the largest group of [Pro]testant worshippers in Britain. Other [Pro]testant Churches include the Methodist [Chu]rch and the Church of Scotland.

The makings of the British

Invasion and settlement

Until about 8000 BC, much of Britain had been covered by ice sheets and glaciers. The few thousand people who arrived there at the end of the last Ice Age were hunters and fishers who used stone and bone tools.

When the ice melted, the sea-level rose and Britain became an island. Settlers who crossed from Europe brought new ways and equipment with them and, from about 3500 BC, the British began to become farmers.

Later settlers introduced another important change: the use of tools made of metal rather than stone. First bronze was used. Then, from around 550 BC, iron was introduced. During this whole period, Britain was being settled by a new group of skilled farmers and fighters who came from Central Europe, called the Celts.

In 55 BC, the Roman leader Julius Caesar made a brief raid on Celtic Britain. But it was not until AD 43, under the Emperor Claudius, that the Romans finally conquered the British Celts. Only the Scottish Highlands remained outside Roman control.

The end of Roman Britain

The rule of the Romans lasted until AD 410, when the Roman troops left. Soon tribes from northern Europe, Angles, Saxons and Jutes, began to invade the eastern part of Britain. The Romanized British fought back but, in the end, they were forced to move westwards into remoter areas such as Wales. Later, in the eighth century, the Anglo-Saxons began to be invaded by the Viking raiders and traders of Scandinavia.

The last invasion came in 1066, when William of Normandy (William the Conqueror) defeated the Saxons and made himself king of England. But Wales did not give in to Norman rule until 1282. Scotland remained a separate kingdom.

▼ In the sunlight again after more than 1600 years: the skeletons of a man (right) and a woman (left) of Roman Britain are examined by an archaeologist in a Roman cemetery at Colchester.

The Romans invade Britain. There were
Roman invasions: Julius Caesar's in
c (shown here), and the invasion of the
peror Claudius in AD 43.

Stonehenge was finally completed by
ut 1750 BC. It is the earliest major work
ritish architecture which has survived.
architects were people who lived
ng Britain's Bronze Age.

▲ A Saxon. After the Romans had
abandoned Britain in the fifth century AD,
Angles and Jutes from Denmark and
Saxons from Germany conquered and
gradually settled the country. The Saxons
started their raids while the Romans were
still in Britain; as defence, Roman forts
were built along the 'Saxon' (or east)
coast.

▲ A Viking of the eighth century AD. The
Vikings are usually depicted as raiders
who later settled and became farmers.
Recently, however, experts have begun to
think that they came to Britain also as
traders, and were quite a sophisticated
people.

▲ A Norman soldier of William the
Conqueror's army. Soldiers like this, who
fought the troops of the Saxon King
Harold, were rewarded with gifts of land
to live in.

The monarchs of Britain

Under one rule

Britain is a monarchy: the headship of state is an office into which the holder is born rather than elected, and which carries the ancient title of 'king' or 'queen'. The British monarchy started in 1603. Originally there were separate rulers for England, Scotland and Wales.

After the Romans left in AD 410, Britain became a collection of small independent kingdoms. The first to bring the English under his rule was Egbert, who died in 839. The monarchy he founded was continued by his successors, such as Alfred the Great. It was continued, too, by the last invader of Britain, William the Conqueror. His family continued to rule for almost a century, after which it was followed by a family that was related by marriage, the Plantagenets. During the Plantagenets' long period in power, Wales was annexed.

Another important development came in 1603. King James VI of Scotland then became King James I of England on the death of Elizabeth I, last of the Tudor monarchs. He first used the title 'King of Great Britain', although there was no union of the Scottish and the English parliaments until 1707.

The monarch's power challenged

First it was the noblemen who tried to challenge the power of the monarch. Later it was Parliament, which voiced the needs of the rich merchants. The biggest challenge came with the Civil War of 1642–8, which led to the execution of King Charles I and the abolition of the monarchy. (It was restored in 1660.) The last monarch to make a serious attempt to control Parliament was George III. Since his death in 1820, British monarchs have 'reigned, but not ruled'. The real power lies with Britain's government, led by the prime minister.

▲ Alfred the Great, king of Wessex in t[he] south and west of England. He ruled at [the] time of the invasions by various groups from Scandinavia, and succeeded in keeping the invaders out of Wessex. Th[e] story that he let a cottager's cakes burn is only a legend.

◀ The Virgin Queen, or 'Good Queen Bess': Elizabeth I of England, greatest o[f] the Tudor monarchs and one of the mos[t] able rulers Britain has ever had. During [her] reign society became more stable, the a[rts] flourished, and England became the foremost power in Europe.

▼ The Royal Standard of Britain (the lions of England, the Welsh harp and the lion of Scotland), and the English coronation regalia, kept in the Tower of London.

The Ampulla

The Sceptre

The Orb

The Anointing Spoon

St. Edward's Crown

▲ At home with the royal family in the eighteenth century: King George III with his wife, Queen Charlotte, and six of their children. George III aimed to recapture the power of the British monarch. For a while he succeeded in ruling through Parliament by bribing his supporters there to do what he wanted.

▼ The British monarch in the twentieth century: Queen Elizabeth II, here seen on tour in the West Indies in 1966. As well as being the sovereign of the United Kingdom of Great Britain and Northern Ireland, she is also head of the Commonwealth.

Mary Stuart, Queen of Scots, Elizabeth['s] cousin and a Catholic. Catholics saw her [as] Elizabeth's rival for the English throne. [She] was thus a source of danger to [Eliza]beth's Protestant government and [Eliza]beth had her executed. But, after [Eliza]beth's death, Mary's son, James VI of [Scot]land, also became England's ruler.

15

The British revolutions

More food for less work

After the Civil War of the 1640s, Great Britain never had another armed revolution similar to that of, for example, France or Russia. But its people led two revolutions of a different sort that changed the lives of almost everyone in the world.

The first one, which started in the late seventeenth century, was a revolution in agricultural methods. Over the next hundred years, British landowners and farmers made enormous strides in producing more food for less work. They did this by, for example, improving the quality of their breeds of livestock, developing new farm machinery and farming systems.

Steam, water and factories

This Agricultural Revolution had two very important effects. Over the years, the growth in food supply meant a growth in population. But farming

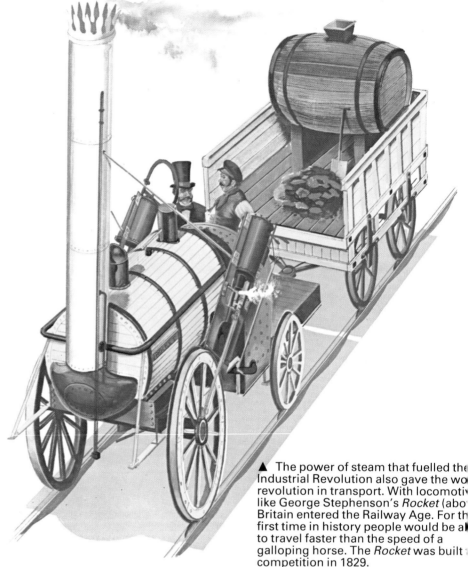

▲ The power of steam that fuelled the Industrial Revolution also gave the wo revolution in transport. With locomoti like George Stephenson's *Rocket* (abo Britain entered the Railway Age. For th first time in history people would be a to travel faster than the speed of a galloping horse. The *Rocket* was built competition in 1829.

now used less labour and fewer people were needed to produce the nation's food. They were therefore free for (and desperately needed) other work.

Improved farming implements were not the only British technological advances of the 1700s. Others were Newcomen's pumping engine run by steam, and Arkwright's spinning machine run on water-power. The harnessing of these two kinds of power to machines led to the growth of 'manufactories', in which goods could be made much more quickly than ever they could by hand. This was the second British revolution.

Although the factories of the Industrial Revolution put many old-style craftsmen out of a job, they gave work to huge numbers of people to whom farming no longer offered a living. They also formed the base on which the wealth of Great Britain and the other industrialized countries of the world would grow.

▲ As the Industrial Revolution gathered pace, its machinery got larger and more powerful. The machine shown here is a hammer worked by steam, the invention of an engineer called James Nasmyth.

◄ The Industrial Revolution brought huge wealth and power to Britain. But to many of the people who laboured in its factories, it also brought appalling working and living conditions; pollution of air, water and land was another of its legacies.

▲ New farming methods made landowners more prosperous; the trim buildings of this village date from Coke's century.

▼ One of Britain's great agricultural reformers: Thomas Coke (pronounced 'Cook'), Earl of Leicester. He owned a large estate in West Norfolk. When he took it over in 1776, it was poor farming land, but he increased its value enormously by improving farming methods.

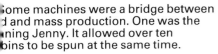

Some machines were a bridge between [han]d and mass production. One was the [spin]ning Jenny. It allowed over ten [bob]bins to be spun at the same time.

Queen-Empress: the age of Queen Victoria

Wealth and power

By the nineteenth century, the powers of the British monarch were more limited than they had been. But, all the same, Queen Victoria acted in the style of a great ruler. Her husband, German-born Prince Albert, tried to do the same, but with less success. The part he played in building up the reputation of the monarchy is recognized today. But the British of his own time never quite accepted him, because he was a foreigner.

Victoria only took the title of Empress – Empress of India – when her reign was halfway over, in 1876. But its splendour reflects the way in which Britain's power and wealth grew throughout the Victorian age.

Social reforms

Victorian Britain is also remembered, though, for its dreadful slums. These were not new to the great cities, but it was in the Victorian period that the press and public leaders first began to notice them. Reformers like Lord Shaftesbury campaigned for the removal of social evils and at the same time the poor themselves were beginning to work for improvements. Education was seen as an important way of achieving social reform, and many schools were built. Although 'Victorian values' are now criticized for their strictness, many changes were taking place behind the scenes.

Victoria herself is often thought of now as a grim old lady. But she was interested in the arts, in helping to spread education, and, according to her own letters, in reducing the power of the aristocracy. (Unlike many other rulers of her period, she was not aristocratic in outlook, and believed that most members of the upper classes were lazy, thoughtless, and immoral.) She loved animals, enjoyed a joke and, given the social climate of her time, she could be surprisingly broad-minded about people or behaviour which her subjects woul have disapproved of.

Her reputation for grimness mai comes from her reaction to Prince Albert's death in 1861. She loved h deeply, and she was so grief-stricke that she hid herself away for severa years. From then on, the image gre of the 'Widow of Windsor', swath in black and completely cheerless.

Throughout most of her long rei she continued to be popular. Wher she died in 1901, the whole nation went into mourning. People felt th both the old queen and the old century were now dead, and Britai and its empire would never be the same again. In fact the empire had yet to reach its greatest extent, and the Edwardian period would be remembered as a golden age. But more huge changes were on the wa

◄ In the early hours of the morning on 20 June 1837, Victoria – then aged 18 – was woken to be told that her uncle, William IV, was dead and that she was now queen. As this picture shows, the scene became a favourite with Victorian artists. Until she was 11, Victoria did not realize she would one day rule Britain. On finding out, she is reported to have said: "I will be good."

▲ During Victoria's reign, British soldie often took part in wars abroad. Among these was the Crimean War against Rus (1854–6). It was during this war that the Charge of the Light Brigade took place. The troops knew the charge would be suicide, but they were ordered to advan regardless. Out of 673 men, 113 were ki and 134 wounded.

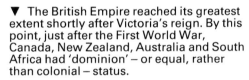

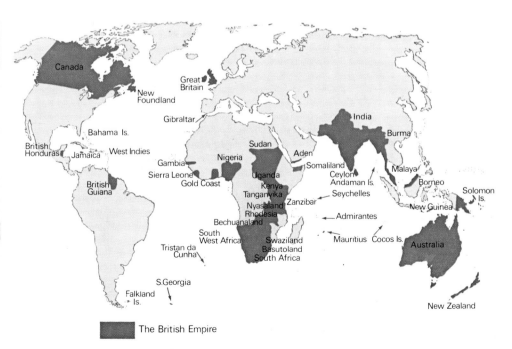

◄ An historic photograph of four British monarchs, showing Victoria with the later Edward VII, George V and Edward VIII.

▲ Poverty in the city slums of Victorian Britain. There was a huge gulf between the rich and the poor. At the poorest level of society children like these not only had no permanent shelter or source of food, they might well have no one at all to care for them. Barefoot and sleeping on the ground in any corner they could find, they spent their days trying to obtain food from wherever they could.

▼ The British Empire reached its greatest extent shortly after Victoria's reign. By this point, just after the First World War, Canada, New Zealand, Australia and South Africa had 'dominion' – or equal, rather than colonial – status.

Britain's influence in the world was [v]ied by other power-seeking countries, [s]hown in this 1880s French cartoon. It [dep]icts British influence over Egypt.

Canada
New Foundland
Great Britain
Gibraltar
Bahama Is.
British Honduras
Jamaica
West Indies
British Guiana
Gambia
Sierra Leone
Gold Coast
Nigeria
Sudan
Aden
Somaliland
India
Burma
Uganda
Kenya
Tanganyika
Nyasaland
Rhodesia
Zanzibar
Ceylon
Andaman Is.
Seychelles
Malaya
Borneo
Solomon Is.
New Guinea
Admirantes
Mauritius Cocos Is.
Australia
Bechuanaland
South West Africa
Swaziland
Basutoland
South Africa
Tristan da Cunha
S.Georgia
Falkland Is.
New Zealand

▨ The British Empire

How Great Britain has changed

Benefiting from the boom

When Queen Victoria died, Britain was still one of the world's great powers. Little more than half a century later, its empire had vanished and its international prestige had been hugely reduced. But, by then, life was better for the vast majority of the British people than it had ever been.

Britain's welfare state – planned during the Second World War and introduced after it – brought together and improved the reforms of earlier periods. These reforms included early versions of unemployment pay and health insurance, along with pensions for the elderly. Both left- and right-wing governments remembered the appalling unemployment of the 1930s, and were determined not to let this return.

In some areas British industry had benefited from wartime inventions, and living standards were improving. Consumer durables like washing machines and television sets had, by the 1960s, come within the reach of average families. Young people also benefited from the economic boom.

Record unemployment

At the start of the 1970s, most people expected their prosperity to continue. But at the same time there was accelerating inflation. The situation was soon made much worse by the oil crisis of 1973, when the oil-producing nations exerted pressure to increase the price of oil. Oil prices soared, and other prices did the same. Industrial demand slackened. In Britain, as elsewhere, there was unemployment on the scale remembered and feared from the 1930s. In Britain, the unemployment figure for January 1986 stood at 3 407 729: the highest ever recorded. The same month, government research suggested that the British were better off 'on average' than they used to be even in the early 1970s. Income levels were up; so was life expectancy. Working hours were down.

But the pattern of Britain's industry had changed (see pages 28–29), and the still-growing army of unemployed people were victims of these changes.

▲ Swinging Sixties, Swinging London Britain's growing affluence had by then dramatically altered the social position its young people. Instead of following t parents' styles, they now created their and, in the 1960s, they set their stamp the world by establishing fashions and styles which were followed internation The best-known shopping centre of the period, Carnaby Street (shown here), is still popular with tourists.

◀ British miners drilling holes for explosives in a coal face. Britain's big c deposits launched the Industrial Revolution. Coal remained Britain's ma fuel until 20 years ago, when cheap oil became a major alternative. Now coal production has fallen to half the 1950 le and an enormous number of miners ha lost their jobs.

▼ Many traditional British industries, such as mining and steel-making, are ir decline. But others are growing and, of these, the new electronics industry is or of the most successful. In the Scottish factory shown here, circuit boards are being tested.

Will I find a job today? Britain, like many industrial countries, is suffering from massive unemployment, and many young people are facing a grim future in which they may never work.

▼ London during bombing raids in the Second World War. St Paul's Cathedral survived, and so did Britain. Afterwards people determined to make a world that was better to live in than the pre-war one.

▲ All lined up and ready to go: cars on the dockside awaiting export. But this dock is not in Britain, one of the traditional homes of the motor industry. It is in Japan – now one of the world's leading manufacturers of motor vehicles. After reaching a peak in 1972, British car manufacture has now dwindled to less than half of its former output, while car imports have shot up. As a result, over 180 000 jobs have been lost to British workers in the industry.

The arts past and present

A literary nation

Britain is a literary nation. There have been important British musical composers, painters and architects, but it is in literature that the British arts have reached their highest point. And, within literature, one man alone has ensured that drama has been Britain's greatest contribution to the world. William Shakespeare lived almost 400 years ago, but the action and excitement of his plays still make a huge impact on audiences everywhere.

The strength of Britain's literary tradition continues today, with more plays being written than can ever be staged. One important outlet for British playwrights is television. Television plays by such writers as Dennis Potter and Alan Bennett are praised all over the world. Televised versions of Shakespeare, and of novels by Trollope and others, have also been much acclaimed. International fame has also greeted the products of Britain's newly-revived film industry, films like *Chariots of Fire* and *Gandhi*.

Passionate admirers

After drama, the novel is the greatest British contribution to the arts. The works of the great nineteenth-century novelists like Charles Dickens, Jane Austen and Thomas Hardy can be read again and again with increasing enjoyment.

The members of another and much older literary tradition are almost as famous. From Chaucer onwards, British poets have inspired deep love and devotion. Donne, Pope, Keats, Shelley, Rupert Brooke, Stevie Smith all have their passionate admirers. And this passion is shared by lovers of two other forms of art: that practised by British painters, from Constable to David Hockney, and by British composers, from Purcell to Benjamin Britten and Michael Tippett.

▲ William Shakespeare (1564–1616). is the nearest we have to an authentic portrait of the playwright. Little is know about his life.

▼ These street performers in London . following a long-standing British tradit in early days, actors also performed ou of-doors, in inn courtyards. Modern str theatre, which turns its back on costly productions and brings drama to casua passers-by, plays a recognized part in t modern British art scene.

◀ Robert Burns (1759–96): farm labourer, customs man and Scotland's national poet. Although renowned even in his own lifetime, he was usually very poor. His fame now extends far beyond Scotland.

▼ A Welsh harpist leads a group of country dancers and singers. Wales has a strong and quite distinct artistic tradition, centring mainly on music and the Welsh language. The national *Eistedfodd* is a festival of Welsh music and poetry.

▲ Joseph Mallord William Turner (1775–1851) used semi-abstract painting techniques to express the forces of nature. As shown in this picture of the *Fighting Téméraire*, he was fascinated by the power and effects of light.

▲ The great Victorian novelist Charles Dickens (1812–1870) created some of the most vividly-drawn characters in English fiction. The best-known of his works is possibly *Oliver Twist*, but *Great Expectations*, *The Pickwick Papers* and *A Christmas Carol* – with its anti-hero, Scrooge – are close runners-up. He fearlessly attacked the attitudes held by the people in power at the time towards the poor, the unfortunate and the vulnerable in society. He even criticized their treatment of criminals.

Heroes of fact and fiction

Britain against Saxon invaders in about AD 516 – to Britain's leader in the Second World War, Winston Churchill. Other great warrior heroes who really lived include Robert the Bruce of Scotland, General Wolfe and Lord Nelson.

The great tradition

At the centre of much British art is the Great British Hero: real-life, legendary, or completely fictional. The British have a rich tradition of heroes, and the heroic qualities they admire include courage, energy, and a willingness to risk all to protect the underdog – the poor, the threatened, or the hopelessly outnumbered. The heroic line stretches from King Arthur – who we think may have defended

Romantic failures

Oddly enough, failure does not stop someone being seen as a hero. An even older hero – or, rather, heroine – than King Arthur is the Celtic queen Boudicca, who tried to throw the Romans out of Britain in AD 61. She lost, but her name is still famous almost 2000 years later. Again, Bonnie Prince Charlie failed in his attempt to win the British crown in 1745. But he is still thought of as a glamorous, romantic figure.

Another sort of British hero is admired for his daring, his style and his quick wits. Robin Hood, the outlaw who robbed the rich to give to the poor, is one sort of heroic thief; so is the highwayman Dick Turpin.

▼ Some of Britain's heroes, like King Arthur, are shadowy figures, half-real and half-legendary. But many others, like the British naval commander, Lord Nelson, belong firmly to the world of fact. Trafalgar Square in London commemorates his last victory and his death in 1805.

◄ When the man who might have been the real King Arthur died, people began to tell a great many stories about him. Some were true, some were not, and some were true but were really about other people. In this way, Arthur is remembered both as a (possibly) real person and as a legendary one. A lot of the best-known tales about the king and his warriors come from the Middle Ages and, as shown here, are about beautiful maidens, witch queens, and knights in shining armour.

◀ Sherlock Holmes, unlike King Arthur, was a fictional figure from the start. He was created in the late Victorian period by Sir Arthur Conan Doyle, and quickly became the most famous detective in all literature. His genius for clue-spotting came from meticulous observation and a remarkable memory. He is shown here vanquishing the Hound of the Baskervilles. In the end, Conan Doyle got tired of Holmes and tried to kill him off. But this horrified Holmes fans so much that the author had to bring his creation back to life. Even today, the great detective is so much admired that some people act as if Holmes really existed. His rather plodding companion, Dr Watson, is also famous.

▲ 'Winnie': Winston Churchill, the most recent of Britain's great hero figures, and Prime Minister during the Second World War. His bulldog image and his determination symbolized the country's will to survive.

▼ The British hero tradition is strong enough to absorb characters from other cultures and make them its own. Mr Punch – another anti-hero we love to hate – started life as Pulcinello, a figure from the sixteenth-century Italian stage. He always dressed in white with a pointed hat.

I'D MOVE, ONLY I'M ONE OF THE GOAL-POSTS!

The Great British Anti-hero, modern version. The deplorable attitudes of toon figure Andy Capp are a long way from the high ideals of King Arthur or Imes. He is lazy, deceitful, work-shy, selfish and – as here – he bullies his wife Flo. (She often bullies him back.) In fact, he belongs to the other British hero tradition: the sly trickster. Andy also represents a stereotyped idea of a northerner.

Inventors and discoverers

The inquisitive urge

It is no surprise that the British, who invented the basic technology that launched the Industrial Revolution, should be famous for inventions in general. They are also famous as discoverers and explorers, working in territory that ranges from unmapped oceans to still-mysterious areas of the human body and its workings.

The inquisitive, exploring urge of the British goes back a long way. In the 1500s, Francis Drake sailed round the world. In the seventeenth century, Henry Hudson gave his name to Hudson Bay in Canada, and William Harvey discovered how blood circulates in the human body. Later in the same century, Isaac Newton discovered the law of gravity.

Travellers' inventions

Many of the British inventions have been in the field of transport, from the chronometer to the railways, and much more recently, the hovercraft. The chronometer was invented by John Harrison. It is the super-accurate clock essential to sailors wanting to calculate their course by the principles of navigation. The first practical steamship, was the Scottish *Charlotte Dundas* of 1801. The first heavier-than-air machine to actually fly was a model glider built in 1804 by George Cayley. (In 1853, his coachman was the first to fly in a heavier-than-air machine.) In 1894, engineer Charles Parsons revolutionized sea travel and steamships by inventing the steam turbine engine. And, through early developments in city transport, London was by then becoming the world's first giant metropolis.

▲ Isaac Newton (1642–1727), using a prism to find out about the properties of light. Newton made many important contributions to scientific knowledge, among them the law of gravity.

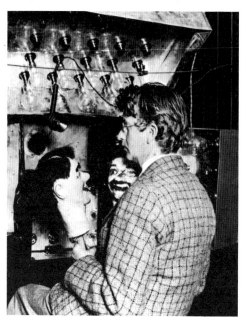

▲ Moving photographs were first shown in the late nineteenth century, but only in the cinema. It was a Scottish engineer, John Logie Baird, who brought them into people's living-rooms. On 26 January 1926, television pictures, transmitted through his mechanical television process, were first demonstrated to scientists. But his system was later scrapped.

► Before the invention of antibiotics, infections were dreaded killers. But, in 1928, Sir Alexander Fleming noticed a mould that had by chance grown in a dish in his laboratory, and that destroyed disease-causing bacteria. He followed up his discovery, and his work led to the development of the first practical antibiotic, penicillin. Others followed, and many killer diseases can now be cured.

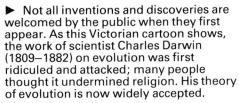
Michael Faraday (1791–1867) made ances in chemistry, physics and ctricity. The genesis of electrical ineering goes back to his discovery of tro-magnetic induction in 1831.

▶ Not all inventions and discoveries are welcomed by the public when they first appear. As this Victorian cartoon shows, the work of scientist Charles Darwin (1809–1882) on evolution was first ridiculed and attacked; many people thought it undermined religion. His theory of evolution is now widely accepted.

▼ The hovercraft is a modern British development in both sea and land travel. Invented by Christopher Cockerell, it moves on a cushion of air and can travel over water or land.

What Britain has to sell

Oil, computers and the 'invisibles'
Britain is a small island with a large urban population. To buy the food and raw materials which it does not produce it must sell its own products abroad, and these mainly take the form of manufactured goods.

In the nineteenth century, when this trading arrangement evolved, Britain was called the 'workshop of the world.' Although later rivalled (and passed) by other countries, it has continued to rely heavily on sales of manufactured goods right up to the present decade. Now, however, its trading pattern has undergone a radical change, and it imports more manufactured goods than it exports. But it also spends less money on food imports than it used to, and less on raw materials. Its fuel imports have gone up but, at the same time, the presence of its own North Sea oil allows it to sell more fuel than it buys.

Although there has been a steep drop in demand for British industry's traditional products (such as steel and textiles, engineering products, cars, ships and aircraft), some areas of work have been growing. One is the computer industry. Others are insurance and banking. Services like banking are part of what is called 'invisible trade' and are an important source of income for Britain. Tourism is another major 'invisible': the millions of people who visit the country each year are buying the experience of being in Britain, using their own countries' money to do so.

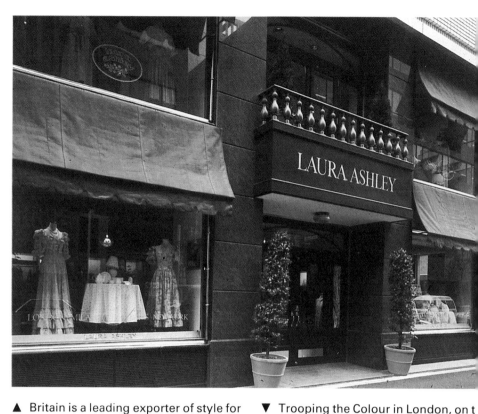

▲ Britain is a leading exporter of style for people of all ages. Laura Ashley clothes, with their reminders of country-house gardens, sell all over the world. This Laura Ashley shop is in New York.

▼ Trooping the Colour in London, on t Queen's official birthday. Pageantry bri millions of tourists to Britain, and earns the country huge sums of money. In 198 alone there were 14,577,000 visitors.

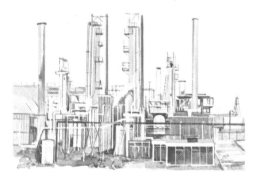

▲ The chemicals industry is a major pillar of the British economy. It has suffered much less from the decline in manufacturing than have the traditional British industries such as textile-making.

▲ Dark-suited 'city gents' throng the floor at London's Stock Exchange. Britain is one of the world's leading financial markets. Handling money transactions brings Britain a lot of foreign business.

▼ All over the world, British pottery is famous for its superb standards of craftsmanship. It is still made in many traditional styles. Here, skilled workers are painting in an intricate design by hand.

▲ Following the discovery of oil in the North Sea, Britain has become an important oil-producing country. But people are worried about what will happen when the oil runs out.

London: the capital city

The founding of London

Britain's capital city, London, was established in the first century AD by the Romans. The new town, which Britain's conquerors called Londinium, grew up on the site of the present City of London. This was the nearest convenient point to the sea where a bridge – the first London Bridge – could be built across the River Thames.

London grew from a small bridgehead settlement into a big city. The river and its bridge brought transport and trade; prestige came when King Edward the Confessor built a palace and an abbey along the river at the neighbouring settlement of Westminster. Once these two settlements had been joined together by buildings, London started growing outwards, taking in many outlying villages on the way. Together with its suburbs, twentieth-century London measures 58 km across, and is the seventeenth biggest city in the world. It now has a population of nearly seven million.

London's violent history

Like many other capital cities, London has had a violent history. It has been attacked or burned several times, the last time during the bombing raids of the Second World War. The most famous London blaze was the Great Fire of 1666, which started in a corner of the city and destroyed nearly all of it. Sir Christopher Wren built the present St Paul's Cathedral to replace the one that was burned.

Things to see in London

1 The Shield of the City of London

2 Trafalgar Square

3 St. Martin-in-the-Fields Church

4 Tower Bridge

5 The Houses of Parliament and Big

6 St. Paul's Cathedral

7 The Tower of London

A Yeoman of the Guard

A Tower Raven

he heart of London today: the City,
the Strand that was its first link with
tminster; the smart districts of
htsbridge and Belgravia; Soho,
us for its restaurants; Oxford Street,
ys thronged with shoppers; the
llectual quarter' of Bloomsbury, home
e British Museum; and five of
lon's parks. Most theatres are sited
een Oxford Street and the Strand.

▲ View of the City of London from the South Bank of the River Thames. The dome of St Paul's Cathedral, masterpiece of the architect Sir Christopher Wren, is dwarfed by modern office blocks.

▼ Leicester Square, in the heart of London's entertainment and nightlife districts. Part of the square is barred to traffic, so people can stroll about freely.

▲ The Serpentine Lake in Hyde Park is close to the very centre of London, but it can make Londoners feel as if they are in the country. London has many parks.

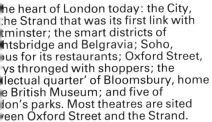

▲ Leather, studs and startling hairstyles are the trademark of London's famous punks. Once seen as threatening, punk styles now attract the attention of tourists and their cameras.

Cloudy skies and green, green gardens

Can we walk on it?

One of the first things summer visitors to Britain notice is the greenness of the landscape. And the sights they look for include the lush, scented gardens that surround many British homes. The British lawn, carefully mown into a pattern of pale and dark green stripes, is especially famous. "Can we walk on it?" is the question visitors often ask, and are delighted that they can. They are also delighted to find grapes ripening under cloudy skies and palm trees on the same latitude as Newfoundland.

Moist, mild and moderate

The reason both for these surprises and for the general fame of Britain's gardens lies in another of Britain's famous features: its weather. Typical British weather is moist and mild. (The warm Gulf Stream current flowing past Britain's west coast helps to keep winter temperatures up.

This moderate climate allows Britain's gardeners to grow plants that come from all over the world, from the Himalayas to the Mediterranean. But the British climate is also very changeable. So gardeners and farmers always have to be ready to protect their more delicate plants from sudden frosts.

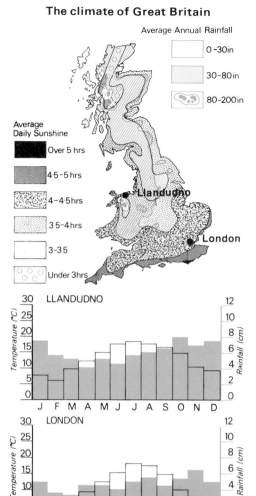

The climate of Great Britain

Average Annual Rainfall

- 0–30in
- 30–80in
- 80–200in

Average Daily Sunshine

- Over 5 hrs
- 4·5–5 hrs
- 4–4·5 hrs
- 3·5–4 hrs
- 3–3·5
- Under 3hrs

Llandudno

London

LLANDUDNO

LONDON

▲ Britain's weather becomes sunnier and drier the further one goes south and east, as shown by the rainfall columns in the two charts.

▲ Prevailing winds over Britain come from the south-west, across the Atlanti and bring plenty of moisture with them usually falls as rain; snow is fairly unus

▼ Spain? In fact, this is a holiday camp in England. In the south, summer temperatures start at around 18°C, and go higher. It is the changeability of the climate, turning to rain with little warni that can be the problem.

▲ The Albert Memorial, commemorating Queen Victoria's husband, in one of the best-loved of London's parks, Kensington Gardens. There are velvety green lawns and sheets of daffodils in March. To do well daffodils need lots of moisture in spring.

◄ The snow-covered north face of Ben Nevis in the north-west of Scotland. It is Britain's highest mountain and stands at 1343 m. above sea level. There can be snow on it for a great part of the year.

▼ Plants from the southern hemisphere grow with palm trees in Inverewe Gardens, even further north than Ben Nevis. But the sea and the warm Gulf Stream current flowing up from the Caribbean keep the climate mild.

Homes and households

Pride in ownership

Home ownership is a British ideal, and the ideal home is usually a house, with its own front door and a garden for children to play in. The number of British homes that are actually owned, rather than rented, by their occupiers has risen sharply since the Second World War and now stands at almost two-thirds of the total. Fewer than a third are rented from local councils, and this number is steadily falling as occupiers buy the council homes that they live in.

Two up, two down

The typical style for older housing in England and Wales is the two-up-two-down terrace: a street of identical houses, each with two rooms on each of its two floors. Streets of terraced houses are found all over the country, built of materials that differ according to the area and age of the street. Many have been enlarged, with a loft extension in the attic. In Scotland the tradition is for apartments, or flats, in large blocks. Another common building style is the semi-detached, two-household home in the suburbs.

A government survey in 1983 showed that over half of British households are made up of married couples and their children. Nearly a quarter of households are made up of single people living on their own.

The British are informal and friendly, as long as their privacy is respected. Their homes are above all places to escape the world outside.

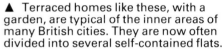

▲ Terraced homes like these, with a garden, are typical of the inner areas of many British cities. They are now often divided into several self-contained flats.

◄ Three years old today: a family meet to celebrate the birthday of a young member. Not every family has a garden but those who do take every opportunit to be out in them – weather permitting.

▲ Shopping – for the day or the week? Supermarkets have revolutionized British shopping habits because of the types of processed and packaged foods they offer. Their prices are often lower than those in smaller shops.

▼ Doing things about the house and garden is a typically British way of spending leisure time. Here, the family car gets its turn.

▼ How the average British household spent its money in 1984. Spending on housing and transport (as a proportion of total household spending) had gone up since the 1960s.

Christmas dinner with roast turkey and :h plum pudding is a traditional British al, and for many families it is one of the n highlights of the year. Festivals are mportant time for family gatherings.

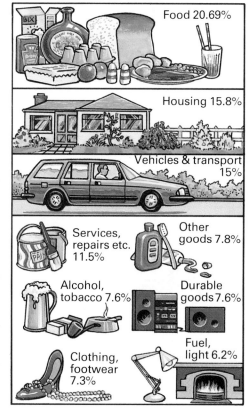

Food 20.69%

Housing 15.8%

Vehicles & transport 15%

Services, repairs etc. 11.5%

Other goods 7.8%

Alcohol, tobacco 7.6%

Durable goods 7.6%

Clothing, footwear 7.3%

Fuel, light 6.2%

Eating the British way

Changing habits

Until recently, British food had an undeserved reputation for dullness. During the war years, many foods were in short supply, and plain food became the norm. However, Elizabethan cookery was famous, and so was that of the Edwardian era at the beginning of our century. But many servants were needed to cook and serve an Edwardian dinner of 12 courses. As fewer people became prepared to be servants, meals began to be simpler.

The basic British cooking tradition relies heavily on foods that are boiled, baked or fried: cakes, puddings, chips and 'bangers-and-mash' (sausages and mashed potato) are some of them. But this tradition is also changing. The British are becoming more health conscious, and more and more people are trying to cut down on the amount of heavy, fatty food they eat. Also very many married women work outside the home as well as look after their families. They often find it easier to buy food that is already prepared and packaged, rather than make traditional dishes.

▶ Like much old-style food, the traditional cheeses of Britain are on the solid side. Cheddar and Stilton are the best known. Others which are easily available are Leicester, Double Gloucester, Derby and Wensleydale. Caerphilly is a mild white hard cheese which originated in Wales. Cheese with pickles and bread makes the modern pub meal known as a 'ploughman's lunch'.

Typical meals for a day

The workday breakfast usually consists of cereals, toast, and tea or coffee.

Lunch is often a quick meal such as sausages and baked beans with tea or coffee.

Evening dinner is the main meal, eaten as early as 6 pm, or much later. A favourite is traditional steak and kidney pie; it can be bought ready-made and frozen.

▼ The cultures meet in this take-away: customers either have a Turkish-style kebab, or follow the British tradition and opt for fish and chips. Ethnic restaurants now flourish, catering for Britain's increasingly varied tastes in food.

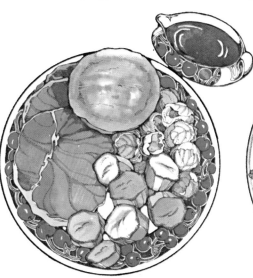

▲ Roast beef, Yorkshire pudding, roast potatoes, and sprouts make up the classic main dish of the traditional Sunday lunch. The 'roast beef of old England' is among the most famous of Britain's dishes; its Yorkshire accompaniment is almost as celebrated.

▲ Haggis is a Scottish speciality. It is made of offal, suet, onions, oatmeal and seasoning, all stuffed into a sheep's stomach, like a giant sausage. It is traditionally served on Burns' Night, when the Scots celebrate their national poet, Robert Burns.

FISH & CHIP

DONER - FISH &

XED VEGETABLE SOUP

kg/1lb mixed vegetables (potato,
nion, turnip, carrot)
g/1 oz fat
tre/2 pints hot stock
soning
g/1 oz oatmeal or rolled oats
ml/¼ pint milk
rsley

op the vegetables finely. Melt the fat
d turn them in it. Add the stock and
soning. Bring to the boil, then simmer
til the vegetables are tender. Then stir in
e oatmeal or rolled oats with milk and
ok, stirring, for ten minutes more. Add
e chopped parsley when serving.

SHEPHERD'S PIE

½ kg/1 lb potatoes
2 teaspoons of milk
knob of butter or margarine
1 chopped onion
dripping or lard
225 g/½ lb cooked minced meat
150 ml/¼ pint hot stock
herbs and seasoning

Boil the potatoes; strain, then mash them,
using milk, butter and seasoning. Fry the
onion in dripping or lard; stir in the minced
meat and fry it lightly; then add the stock,
seasoning and herbs. Put the meat mixture
in a pie dish and cover it with mashed
potato. Make a pattern in the potato with a
fork, add a few flakes of butter or
margarine, and heat it in a medium oven
for half an hour.

BAKED APPLES AND CUSTARD

4 large cooking apples
1 tablespoon golden syrup
25 g/1 oz brown sugar
50 g/2 oz dried fruit
Wash the apples and cut out the cores,
using an apple corer or small knife. Fill the
hole in each apple with syrup, sugar and
dried fruit. Place in a greased dish with a
little water and bake in a medium oven
until tender.

Custard

2 tablespoons custard powder
25 g/1 oz sugar, ½ litre/1 pint cold milk
few drops vanilla essence
Make the custard, following the
instructions on the packet. Serve with the
baked apples.

▲ Britain is an island nation, and seafood
forms an important part of the British diet.
Shellfish are cheap and nutritious, so
whelks, cockles, mussels and eels are all
among the traditional foods of London's
East End. Whelk stalls are now also a
tourist attraction.

Education in Britain

Universal education

British parents are required by law to see that their children receive efficient full-time education between the ages of 5 and 16. For all parents who wish it, this education is 'free': that is, it is provided as a public service, and paid for through taxation.

This free system of education – which, of course, is paid for by all rate- and tax-payers, whether they are parents or not – is usually called the 'state system', and dates back to the late nineteenth century. (Free elementary education for almost all children was introduced in 1891.)

It exists alongside the separate, and much smaller, system of independent schools, for which most pupils' parents pay fees. The independent system includes such famous 'public schools' as Eton and Harrow. In 1984 there were just under nine million pupils in state schools, and half a million in independent schools.

In state schools in England and Wales, pupils usually move from primary to secondary school when they are 11. (In Scotland – which has a separate system – they move up at 12.) Until the 1970s, most pupils sat an exam called the 11-plus, which decided what sort of secondary school they went to. Only the brightest were allowed to go on to an academic education. Today, almost all pupils in the state system throughout Great Britain go to the same sort of secondary school: the comprehensive. This takes children of all abilities.

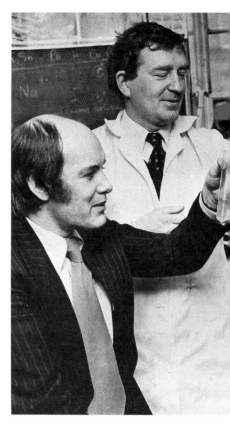

▲ A science lesson taking place in a Scottish secondary school. The Scottish education system is slightly different from that of England and Wales.

◀ Plenty of room to play in this modern urban primary school. Primary education is a child's first experience of formal schooling; teaching methods integrate both play and study.

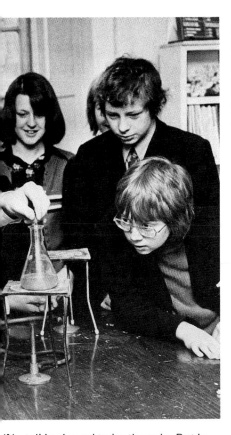

'No talking' used to be the rule. But in [sch]ools today, like this secondary one, [dis]cussion is encouraged and pupils can [con]sult the teacher and each other.

[S]tudents at Cambridge University. In [198]3, 292,000 young people went on after [sch]ool to study full-time at universities. In [Eng]land alone, almost two million more [wen]t to other sorts of colleges.

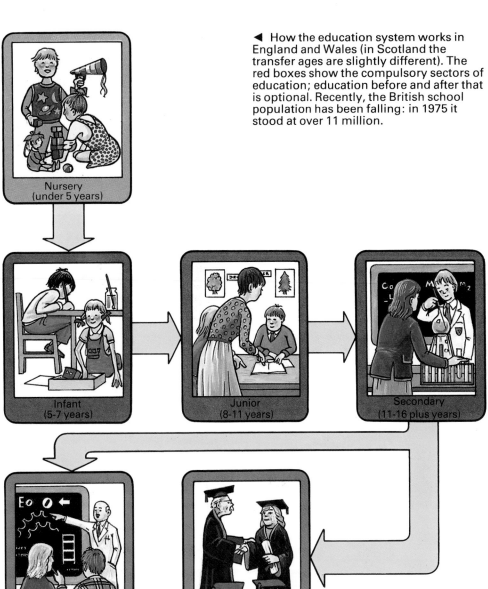

◄ How the education system works in England and Wales (in Scotland the transfer ages are slightly different). The red boxes show the compulsory sectors of education; education before and after that is optional. Recently, the British school population has been falling: in 1975 it stood at over 11 million.

Nursery
(under 5 years)

Infant
(5-7 years)

Junior
(8-11 years)

Secondary
(11-16 plus years)

(16 plus years)
Further education

(18 plus years)
University

Time off: leisure and pleasure

Home-based pursuits

The average working week in Britain is now 37–38 hours. Although several hours' travelling time should be added to this total, it still allows the British a good amount of leisure time. How do they like spending their time off?

Although a wide variety of leisure pursuits is available – from grand opera for London-dwellers to walking in the countryside – a few favourites have topped the list for well over ten years. Topmost of all is watching television: in a government survey in 1983, at least 97 per cent of the people asked said they had watched television in the previous month. Other favourites are also home-based: gardening, listening to tapes or records, doing up the house and – for many women – needlework and

knitting. Going down to the pub is another popular leisure activity (especially for men). But going out for a meal is seen as a luxury.

The great outdoors

In Britain, the countryside is almost always within reach, and 61 per cent of households have a car. But people are less keen on going out in it than they used to be.

Thanks to television, many outdoor sports are also enjoyed indoors, from the hugely popular football to sheepdog trials. But the new interest in health has meant that Britain does go outdoors for pursuits like walking and jogging.

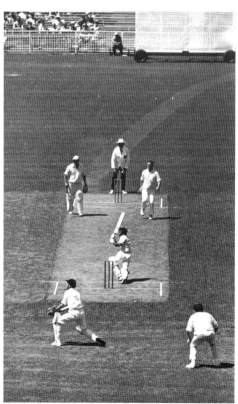

▲ Cricket is sometimes called the English national game; it is certainly one of Britain's greatest and most popular exports to the rest of the world. In Britain itself, it is known to have been played in some form from about the middle of the sixteenth century. Some games can take up to five days, although one-day matches are also played.

Shopping for necessities can be a ...ore, but shopping for leisure equipment ... favourite pastime for the whole family. ...re, even the baby seems intrigued by ... electronic games.

▲ Contestants for the snooker world championships line up for the television cameras. After walking, snooker is the next most popular sport among British men.

▼ A British 'pub' or public house, for centuries a centre for relaxation and entertainment. The attractions include good beer and cheerful companionship.

...Over a quarter of British holiday-...kers go abroad for their holidays. ...nong those who stay, active holidays ...ch as camping, boating and walking are ...at favourites.

...A rugby football match between Wales ... the red shirts – and Japan. Rugby is ...ther of Britain's important sports.

Reference

FACTS AND FIGURES

The land and people
Full title: United Kingdom of Great Britain and Northern Ireland.
Position: Between 50°N and 60°N and 2°E and 8°W. Largest island of Europe, lying north-west of the continent of Europe. Closest neighbours are France, Belgium and the Netherlands.
Constituent parts: Great Britain comprises England, Scotland and Wales. The United Kingdom also includes Northern Ireland. The Isle of Man and the Channel Islands are not strictly part of the UK, but are dependencies of the Crown.
Area: England, 130 367 sq km (50 335 sq miles), Scotland 78 772 sq km (30 414 sq miles), and Wales 20 764 sq km (8011 sq miles).
Population: (1981) England 46 362 836; Scotland 5 130 735; Wales 2 791 851.
Capital: London, pop 6 776 000 (1981).
Language: English, but in Wales 503 559 (1981) spoke Welsh. In Scotland at the same date 79 307 spoke Gaelic.
Religions: Church of England (Protestant Episcopal), approx.1 700 000 members (1982). Church of Scotland, approx. 900 000 members (1983). Methodist Church, 487 000 members (1984). Roman Catholic Church, approx. 5 000 000 (1984). Jewish, approx. 354 000 (1984).
Political system: Constitutional monarchy. Continuous monarchy from 802, except for Commonwealth 1649–60. Supreme legislative authority is the Queen in Parliament (the Queen and the two Houses of Parliament). Constitution unwritten.
Head of State: Her Majesty Queen Elizabeth II, Head of the Commonwealth and Defender of the Faith.
Armed Forces: (1984) 325 100; Army 161 000; Navy 71 000; Air Force 93 000. The USA has air and naval bases in Britain.
International organizations: Member of the United Nations, the Commonwealth, the European Economic Community (EEC), the North Atlantic Treaty Organization (NATO), and the Organization for Economic Cooperation and Development (OECD).

The unwritten constitution
The British system of government has evolved through many hundreds of years. It has been changed constantly to meet changing requirements. The sovereign once had complete power, but is now said to 'reign but not rule'. The UK is governed by her Majesty's Government *in the name of the Queen*.

The two Houses
The British Parliament consists of two parts: the House of Lords and the elected House of Commons. Their job is the same: to pass laws, to make finance available and to put important issues before the electorate. But the Commons, which is elected by almost all citizens over 18 years, is the real seat of parliamentary power.

The Government
The political party which has the most Members of the House of Commons elected in a general election, forms the government. Its leader becomes the Prime Minister and chooses the members of the government. The most important ministers form the Cabinet which makes government policy. But the Cabinet must have the support of its party both in Parliament and the country.

History

Kings and Queens of England
Saxons and Danes

802–39	Egbert
839–58	Ethelwulf
858–60	Ethelbald
860–6	Ethelbert
866–71	Ethelred
871–99	Alfred the Great
899–924	Edward the Elder
924–40	Aethelstan
940–6	Edmund
946–55	Edred
955–9	Edwy
959–75	Edgar
975–8	Edward the Martyr
978–1016	Ethelred the Unready
1016	Edmund Ironside
1016–35	Canute the Dane
1035–40	Harold I
1040–2	Harthacnut
1042–66	Edward the Confessor
1066	Harold II

House of Normandy

1066–87	William I (the Conqueror)
1087–1100	William II
1100–35	Henry I
1135–54	Stephen

House of Plantagenet

1154–89	Henry II
1189–99	Richard I (Lionheart)
1199–1216	John
1216–72	Henry III
1272–1307	Edward I
1307–27	Edward II
1327–77	Edward III
1377–99	Richard II

House of Lancaster

1399–1413	Henry IV
1413–22	Henry V
1422–61	Henry VI

House of York

1461–83	Edward IV
1483	Edward V
1483–5	Richard III

House of Tudor

1485–1509	Henry VII
1509–47	Henry VIII
1547–53	Edward VI
1553–8	Mary Tudor (Mary I)
1558–1603	Elizabeth I

House of Stuart

1603–25	James I
1625–49	Charles I
[1649–60]	**Commonwealth** (No king)
1660–85	Charles II
1685–8	James II
1689–94	William III and Mary II
1694–1702	William III
1702–14	Anne

House of Hanover

1714–27	George I
1727–60	George II
1760–1820	George III
1820–30	George IV
1830–7	William IV
1837–1901	Victoria

House of Saxe-Coburg

1901–10	Edward VII

House of Windsor

1910–36	George V
1936	Edward VIII
1936–52	George VI
1952–	Elizabeth II

Scottish Kings and Queens 1057–160

1057–93	Malcolm III (Canmore)
1093	Donald Ban
1094	Duncan II
1094–7	Donald Ban (restored)
1097–1107	Edgar
1107–24	Alexander I
1124–53	David I
1153–65	Malcolm V (The Maiden)
1165–1214	William I
1214–49	Alexander II
1249–86	Alexander III
1286–90	Margaret, Maid of Norwa
1292–6	John Baliol
1306–29	Robert I (Bruce)
1329–71	David II
1371–90	Robert II ('the Steward')
1390–1406	Robert III
1406–37	James I
1437–60	James II
1460–88	James III
1488–1513	James IV
1513–42	James V
1542–87	Mary
1587–1625	James VI (became king o England 1603)

dex

...bers in **heavy** type refer to
...rations and captions

...cultural Revolution 16, 17
...aft 26, 28
...t, Prince 18
...d, King 14, **14**
...es 12, 13
...wright 16
...d forces 42
...ur, King 24, **24**, 25
...and artists 22, 23, 24

...l, John Logie 26
...ing 28
...Nevis 8, **9**, 33
...ingham 11
...icca 24
...ze Age 12, 13
...s, Robert 23, 36

...ar, Julius 12, **12**, 13
...bridge University **39**
...o, Andy and Flo **25**
...ey, George 26
...brations 34
...s 10, 12, 24
...nel Islands 42
...nicals industry 28
...stianity 10, **10**, 11
...rchill, Winston 24, **25**
... War 14, 16
...dius, Emperor of Rome
..., 12, 13
...ate 32, **32**, 33
...20
...kerell, Christopher 27
...e, Thomas 17
...monwealth 15
...posers 22
...puters 28
...an Doyle, Arthur **25**
...wall 8, 9
...ntryside 8, 40, 41
...ket 40
...ean War 18

...ce 23
...win, Charles, 27
...on 8
...ens, Charles 22, 23
...overers 26
...e, Francis 26
...na 22, **22**, 25

...Anglia 9
...nomy 28, **28**, 29
...cation 18, **38**, 38, 39
...ardian age 18, 36
...dfodd **23**
...tronics industry 20
...abeth I, Queen 14, **14**, 15

Elizabeth II, Queen 10, 11, 15, 28, 29
Elizabethan age **14**, 36
Empire, British 18, **19**, 20
Engineering industry 28
England 8, 9, 14, 15, 34, 36, 38, 39, 42
Entertainment 22, **22**, 23, 31, 40, **41**
Europe 12, **14**
Explorers 26
Exports *see* Trade

Factories 16, 17
Faraday, Michael 27
Farmers and farming 12, 13, 16, 17
Fashion 20, 28
Fenland 9
Festivals 34, 35
Films 22, 40
First World War **19**
Fleming, Alexander 26, 27
Food 16, 36, **36**, 37, 40
Football 40
Fuel 20

Gardens 32, 33, 34, 35, 40
George III, King 14, **15**
George V, King **19**
Glencoe 8
Government 14, 15, 42
Great Fire of London 30
Gulf Stream 32, 33

Hadrian's Wall **9**
Hargreaves, James **16**
Harold, King 13
Harrison, John 26
Heroes, 24, **24**, 25
Hinduism 10
Holidays **41**
Holmes, Sherlock **25**
Holy Island (Lindisfarne) 9
Homes 34, **34**, 35
Housing 34, **34**, 35
Hovercraft 26, 27

Ice Age 12
Immigration 10, 11
Imports *see* Trade
Industrial Revolution 16, **16**, 17, 20, 26
Industry 16, 20, **20**, 21, 28, **28**, 29
Inflation 20
Invasions and invaders 12, **12**, 13, 14, **14**, 24
Inventors 26, **26**, 27
Inverewe Gardens **33**
Insurance industry 28
Islam 10, **11**
Isle of Man 42

James VI of Scotland and I of England 14, 15
Jutes 12, 13

Kent 9

Language 10, **11**, 42

Leicester Square 31
Leisure 22, 40, **40**, 41
Lincolnshire 9
Literature 22, 23, 24
Loch Ness 9
London 8, 11, 20, 24, 30, **30**, 31, 42
London, City of 30, **30**, 31

Machinery 16, **16**, 17, 26
Mary Stuart, Queen of Scots 15
Medicine 26, 27
Middle Ages 24
Miners 20
Monarchy 14, **14**, 15, 18, **18**, 19, 24, 30, 42
Motor industry 21, 28
Mountains 8, **8**, 9, 33
Music 22, 23
Muslims 11

Nasmyth, James **16**
Nelson, Horatio 24, **24**
Newcomen 16
Newton, Isaac 26, **26**
Norfolk 9, 17
Normans 13
Northern Ireland 8, 15, 42
North Sea 9, 28, **29**

Oil 9, 20, **20**, 28, 29
Oxford University 9

Painters 22, 23
Parks 31, 33
Parliament 14, 30, 42
Parsons, Charles 26
Plantagenets 14
Playwrights 22
Poets 22, 23
Pollution 17
Population 8, **8**, 10, 16, 28, 30, 42
Pottery 9, **29**
Protestants 10, 11, 15, 42
Public houses (Pubs) 40, **41**
Punch, Mr **25**
Punks 31

Railways 16, 26
Religions 10, 11, 15, 42
Rocket 16
Roman Catholics 10, 11, 15, 42
Romans 9, 12, **12**, 13, 14, 24, 30
Royal regalia 15
Royalty *see* Monarchy
Rugby football **41**
Rulers 14
Russia 18

St Andrew's Cross **9**
St Martin's in the Fields Church 30
St Paul's Cathedral **21**, 30, **30**, 31
Saxons 12, 13, 24
Scandinavians 12, **14**
Science 26, **26**, 27, **38**, 39

Scotland 8, **8**, 9, 12, 14, 15, 20, 23, 24, 33, 36, 38, **38**, 39, 42
Second World War 10, 20, 21, **21**, 24, 25, 30, 34
Settlement and settlers 10, 11, 12, **13**
Ships 26, 28
Shopping 31, 35, 40, **41**
Snooker **41**
Social conditions 17, 18, 19, 20, 23, 34, 35, **35**
Social reforms 18, 20
Sport 40, **40**, 41
Staffordshire 9
Steampower 16, **16**, 26
Steel industry 20, 28
Stephenson, George **16**
Stonehenge 13
Stratford 9
Suffolk 9
Sussex 9

Tartans **9**
Technology 16, **16**, 17, 26
Television 20, 22, **26**, 40, **41**
Textiles 28, **28**
Thames, River 30, 31
Theatres 31
Tools 12
Tourism 8, 9, 28, **28**, 29, 31
Tower Bridge 30
Tower of London 30
Towns 8
Trade 13, 21, 28
Trafalgar Square **24**, 30
Transport 8, **16**, 21, 26, 27, 40
Travellers 26
Tudors 14, **14**
Turner, Joseph Mallord William **23**

Unemployment 20, **20**, 21

Victoria, Queen 18, **18**, 19, 20
Victorian age 18, **18**, 19, 23, 25, 27
Vikings 12, 13

Wales 8, 9, 12, 14, 15, 23, 34, 36, 38, 39, **41**, 42
Warwickshire 9
Weather 32, **32**, 33
Welfare State 20
Westminster 30, **30**, 31
William the Conqueror 12, 13, 14
Work *see* Industry, Unemployment
Wren, Christopher 30, 31
Writers 22, 23

ORKNEY
Kirkwall
Thurso
John o' Groats
Wick
SHETLAND
Lerwick

ATLANTIC OCEAN

58

ORKNEY
Kirkwall
Thurso
John o' Groats
Wick
On same scale as m

60

56

WESTERN ISLES

Stornoway
Lairg
Helmsdale
Ullapool
Golspie
Invergordon
Portree
Dingwall
Elgin
Banff
Fraserburgh
Kyle of
Lochalsh
Nairn
Peterhead
Inverness
GRAMPIAN
Mallaig
HIGHLAND
Aberdeen
Kingussie
Ballater
Stonehaven
Fort William
Blair Atholl
Kinlochleven
TAYSIDE
SCOTLAND
Forfar
Oban
Perth
Dundee
Arbroath
Kinross
CENTRAL
Cupar
FIFE
Lochgilphead
Stirling
Kinross
Kirkcaldy
Greenock
Dumbarton
Edinburgh
Rothesay
Paisley
Glasgow
LOTHIAN
Haddington
Campbeltown
Motherwell
Berwick-on-Tweed
STRATHCLYDE
Peebles
Duns
Kilmarnock
Selkirk
Ayr
BORDERS
Sanquhar
Hawick
Alnwick
Moffat
NORTHUMBERLAND

NORTH SEA

56

ATLANTIC OCEAN

DUMFRIES & GALLOWAY
Dumfries
Newcastle
South Shields
Stranraer
Gateshead
TYNE & WEAR
Sunderland
Kirkcudbright
Carlisle
Durham
Hartlepool
Wigtown
Penrith
Appleby
DURHAM
CLEVELAND
Whitehaven
Teesside
Middlesbrough
CUMBRIA
Darlington
Northallerton
Kendal
NORTH YORKSHIRE
Scarborough
Barrow
Lancaster
Harrogate

Londonderry
Coleraine
Lifford
NORTHERN
Ballymena
Larne
Donegal
IRELAND
Antrim
Omagh
Bangor
Enniskillen
Belfast
Downpatrick
Ballina
Sligo
ISLE OF
MAN
Douglas
Carrick-on-Shannon
Cavan
Dundalk

54

North Channel

54

IRISH SEA

York
Longford
Drogheda
LANCASHIRE
Keighley
HUMBERSIDE
Roscommon
Balbriggan
Blackpool
Preston
Bradford
Leeds
Beverley
Hull
An Uaimh
Blackburn
Huddersfield
Athlone
Mullingar
St. Helens
Bolton
Oldham
Barnsley
Doncaster
Scunthorpe
Galway
MERSEYSIDE
Salford
Grimsby
Tullamore
Holyhead
Birkenhead
Manchester
Sheffield
DUBLIN
Llandudno
Liverpool
Chesterfield
Lincoln
Dun Laoghaire
Rhyl
CHESHIRE
Matlock
Birr
Bray
Bangor
Flint
Chester
Crewe
NOTTS
LINCOLN
Port Laoise
Kildare
Caernarvon
CLWYD
DERBY
Mansfield
Ennis
Wicklow
Mold
Nottingham
Boston
GWYNEDD
Stoke-on-Trent
Derby
Nenagh
Carlow
SHROPSHIRE
Sleaford
Arklow
Dolgellau
STAFFORD
Kings Lynn
Shrewsbury
Stafford
NORFOLK

52

Cardigan
ENGLAND
LEICESTER
Welshpool
Walsall
Norwich
Aberystwyth
Wolverhampton
Leicester
Oakham
Peterborough
Bay
Birmingham
4
Ely
CAMBRIDGE
POWYS
Coventry
NORTH-
Cardigan
Kidderminster
Rugby
AMPTON
Bury St. Edmunds
HEREFORD &
WARWICK
Northampton
Cambridge
SUFFOLK
Llandrindod
WORCESTER
Warwick
Bedford
Ipswich
Wells
Worcester
BEDFORD
Cardigan
Hereford
Buckingham
Colchester
Harwich
Fishguard
DYFED
Brecon
Gloucester
OXFORD
BUCKS
Luton
HERTS
ESSEX
Carmarthen
Monmouth
Oxford
Aylesbury
Chelmsford
Haverfordwest
Llanelli
GWENT
GLOUCESTER
Hertford
Pembroke
Merthyr Tydfil
Cwmbran
Watford
WALES
Rhondda
Newport
AVON
Swindon
Reading
Slough
LONDON
Southend
Swansea
Cardiff
Bristol
BERKSHIRE
Gillingham
Margate
Bath
Guildford
Maidstone
Canterbury
Bristol Channel
WILTSHIRE
SURREY
Reigate
KENT
Ilfracombe
Trowbridge
EAST
Dover
HAMPSHIRE
Barnstaple
Wells
WEST SUSSEX
SUSSEX
SOMERSET
Salisbury
Winchester
Hastings
Yeovil
Chichester
Lewes
Bude
Southampton
Brighton
Eastbourne
DEVON
DORSET
Bournemouth
Worthing
Newport
Portsmouth
Dorchester
Poole
Exeter
Weymouth
ISLE OF WIGHT
CORNWALL
Torquay
Plymouth
Torbay
Truro
St. Austell
English Channel
Penzance
Falmouth

Dieppe
FRAN
Abbeville

52

St. George's Channel

ENGLAND, SCOTLAND
& WALES : Political

Cities and Towns
International Boundaries
Internal Boundaries
County & Regional
Boundaries
Railways   Airports
Motorways   Canals
Counties indicated by numbers in England
1 GREATER MANCHESTER   4 WEST MIDLANDS
2 WEST YORKSHIRE   5 WEST GLAMORGAN
3 SOUTH YORKSHIRE   6 MID GLAMORGAN
                        7 SOUTH GLAMORGAN
Scale 1:3,700,000
0   20   40   60 miles
0   40   80 kilometres
Projection : Conical with 2 standard parallels

West from Greenwich 0 East from Greenwich

10   8   6   4   2   0

ENGLAND, SCOTLAND & WALES : Physical

Cities and Towns

International Boundaries

Internal Boundaries

Mountain Peaks ▲ 1887 metres

feet		metres
3000		914
1000		305
500		152
0		0

Scale 1:3,700,000

0   20   40   60 miles

0   40   80 kilometres

Projection : Conical with 2 standard parallels

Un same scale as main map

West from Greenwich 0 East from Greenwich